WHAT IS YOUR PURPOSE?

God Has a plan. You have a purpose!

Jaquan Kline

Studio Griffin
A Publishing Company
www.studiogriffin.net

For information, contact:
Studio Griffin
A Publishing Company
Garner, North Carolina
studiogriffin@outlook.com
www.studiogriffin.net

Cover and Jacket Design by Jaquan Kline
Image; and Cover and Jacket Fonts by © Marketplace Designers
at Canva

First Edition

ISBN-13: 978-1-954818-29-3

Library of Congress Control Number: 2022902828

1 2 3 4 5 6 7 8 9 10

For my loving wife, who reminded me that the gifts
and talents God has given me was not for me
but for the benefit of others, to you I can never
express the depth of my appreciation.

For my parents, who've invested in me in
more ways than one could imagine.

For my daughter, who loves me in a way
that pushes me to be greater.

For my grandmother, who's encouraged
me at my lowest points.

To my siblings, this is to show you God
can use all of us.

TABLE OF CONTENTS

INTRODUCTION

I don't want you to think this book only applies to someone who knows Jesus. This book is for everyone and anyone regardless of their background, ethnicity, or religious preferences. Yes, I consider myself a follower of Jesus, but he was a lover of people. I know that we are all designed with purpose. There's a scripture in the Bible that states:

> *Thank you for making me so wonderfully complex! Your workmanship is marvelous—how well I know it. Psalms 139:14 (NLT)*

We all have our own complexities, but the good news is we were made that way. Diversity is the foundation of creation, and no one individual or one set of thoughts was meant to be highlighted above another. It is my heart's hope that this book will help you navigate through even the most difficult of circumstances and that you may identify purpose in it all. I know we as people don't know much of what we don't know. Many of the things I highlight in this book will give further insight, but it is still up to you to place those things into practice.

I am elated that you have considered this book a worthy read, and I'm certain that you will get something out of it. Do me a favor? Please share this with someone you love dearly or anyone you feel may be struggling with understanding their own path in life. We've only gained our position in life because of someone else's shared resources, so please become a resource for someone else. Enjoy the read!

Part 1:
DISCOVERING PURPOSE

Discovering Purpose

The date was June 30, 2017. I sat in the middle of my cramped, one-bedroom, 640 square foot apartment with a broken A/C unit in the heat of the summer. I had one piece of furniture (a television) and clothes. My space was bare, I didn't have much, and I lived in an impoverished community. My neighbors argued day and night and even got into physical altercations. One night, someone was stabbed outside of my door. Children often roamed the hallways, where a stench of urine constantly lingered. Nomads slept under the staircase or walked throughout the building in the early morning hours until midday. 'Commotion' was the perfect descriptor for all that we encountered as tenants. There was only one entrance into the building as well as one exit. This was symbolic of what I felt about my present circumstances at the time: limited. I felt isolated, as if there were no other obtainable goals within my reach due to how bound I felt by my mental angst.

As a twenty-two-year-old, that's a world of pressure to be under but, the reality is many individuals feel the same way—some young, some old. My life felt as if it had come to a screeching halt, and I was so unfulfilled with all that I'd involved myself in. I'd entered college straight from high school, joined a leadership group, worked for the Governor then a tech company, and even successfully ventured into my own business endeavors, working in high schools, and facilitating life skills workshops.

To those around me, it seemed as though I had certain notable successes. I'd been places and done things. But the truth was, I was a serial starter. There were a host of things I'd begun or even initiated but never saw through to completion. For a variety of reasons, it either became too difficult, I got discouraged, or more importantly, I didn't want to fail. Failure to me was associated with worthlessness. I had such a negative perspective on failure. It symbolized defeat. It even meant I had no value.

While sitting on the living room floor, I'd decided my fate in a matter of thirty minutes. Everyone I knew was graduating college on time, moving into a spacious apartment in a nicer part of town, and being publicly recognized for their accomplishments. Some of them were even in what seemed to be healthy and thriving relationships. So, what was my criteria for success? My meaning for life, my vision, my purpose? I was still asking myself the age-old question, "What is my purpose?"

At this particular stage of my life, purpose was 'career' or 'direction.' Because I had no clear direction for my future, I immediately felt that I had no purpose, no insight for my path in life. I wanted to be an attorney, an entrepreneur, a public speaker, and I had a passion for poetry at the time. How was I supposed to navigate between all those things? If I was meant to just accomplish one thing, then why was it that my desires were all over the place?

For example, I have a younger cousin whom I admire

dearly. She's known since almost her sophomore year of high school that she wanted to be a doctor, and she pursued that. Her husband, a childhood best friend of mine, knew he wanted to be an architect before he even arrived at college. He received a master's degree in architectural engineering.

I often assumed that because I didn't have a similar path for myself, I didn't know my purpose. From the time we enter elementary school until the day we enter college, we are asked, "So what do you want to do when you get older?" Or "What do you want to do when you finish school?" These sorts of questions set us all on a path of expectancy for how our futures should pan out and what they should look like. Unfortunately, these questions never prepare us for the in-between moments or the many uncertainties that we go through while headed on this journey.

I never imagined that there would be moments where I asked myself, "Do I really want to do this?" Moments where I was so conflicted that I went into depression for feeling so unaccomplished. In many ways, my future was shaped even before I had a chance to decide what I wanted to pursue.

Early Beginnings

Most of us have done a few things that we aren't that proud of in our life. For some of us, this occurs in our twenties, maybe even a later age than that. Truthfully, we may always be susceptible to making choices that we hope we never have to acknowledge.

In January of 2011, I found myself in a similar situation. I was seventeen, and I decided I didn't want to live in my parents' home anymore. Like most teens, I thought my parents were 'controlling' and didn't let me do anything I wanted. I constantly felt they didn't understand me, and thought it'd be better if I was on my own. My father often said, "If you don't like it, then you can find somewhere else to go." Although this wasn't a literal expression, I convinced myself it was. I was being overly dramatic.

One thing about teenage hormones is that they magnify your emotions, making everyone else seem 'crazy' and you the only 'sane' person in your world. At that age, you never think to yourself, "Maybe I'm just having a bad day." Instead, it's, "This is the worst day of my life!" and that person is the cause of it.

My parents and I had been arguing for most of my teenage experience. I wanted to date, but I wasn't allowed to. I wanted to go with my friends, but I wasn't allowed to. I wanted to go to parties, but I wasn't allowed to. I was a caged animal, or so I thought. How dare my parents have morals and standards? How dare they care about my wellbeing? Dating? What did they know? They probably had an arranged marriage.

For the average teenager, living on their own seems like a dream come true—no limitations, no parental supervision—pretty much, no worries at all. Most adolescents have a carefree mentality. They aren't concerned with the consequences of their actions (at least, not in the same regard that older adults are). Youth typically possess a free mindset, a sort of 'so what' attitude. 'Que sera, sera'—whatever will be, will be.

Chores

They are a never-ending job that we all have for a lifetime. I was sick of chores; I was sick of being told when I had to do them and how I had to do them. My thought process was: 'I'm almost a senior, that's basically an adult. Why can't they do it themselves?' This kind of internal dialogue happens in the mind of every teenager. Really, any adolescent living under the roof of their parents' home.

To make matters worse, I wasn't even living in my parents' home—I was at my aunt's house, yet I was still responsible for chores. Technically, I wasn't her child, so her children should have been responsible for their own chores. Selfish? I know, right? But aren't most teens? Show me a teen that's not self-indulged, and I'll show you a problem-free world in return.

All my life, we'd lived in apartments. Once, we stayed in a duplex, but it still felt like an apartment. My parents desired a home of their own, something we could all feel belonged to us. Finally, their dreams came true, and we just had to wait on the closing date. With the school year right around the corner and our new home being in a completely different school district, my parents thought it'd be ideal for me to live at my aunt's for a while. This way, I'd still be in the same school district, and my cousins and I would be able to ride the bus together.

In the beginning, like all new experiences, it was love at first sight. Five boys living together is busy, never a dull moment. And there's always a mess waiting to be cleaned somewhere. Chores were constantly needing to be done. Coming from an only child home to this new world was difficult to adjust to at times. I'd enough of it.

There were a few pros to this situation. For instance, now that I was no longer under my parent's supervision, I had the chance to date. I was able to attend events with my peers. All around it seemed that I had a new level of freedom. This brief stint of freedom lasted all but a couple of months before my aunt told my parents the truth about my lack of effort around the home and my lack of communication of my whereabouts after school. My parents, being as involved as they were, came to the house to have a talk with me and to make sure I understood that even under another roof, I was still expected to abide by the same rules I had at home and to uphold the same standards.

Then the moment came when my father once again said, "If you can't listen to these rules, you need to find somewhere else to go."

I thought to myself, 'Even when I'm not living with him, he's still trying to control me? I don't have to take this.' Then I responded, "I found somewhere to go."

You could feel the tension seep through your pores. It was so thick.

Now ideally, the way that teens think is heavily

contingent upon the benefits they experience. Most adolescents are absent from adult responsibility. The ones that do have more adult-like responsibilities still share the desire to be free from restraint. A teenager struggles with the dubious task of having to submit to authority while realizing the access to the authority they could possess. It's like a president taking orders from the governor—both have authority, but one hasn't quite reached the status of being fully in charge. As many teens struggle with the concept of balancing life and submission, they are often led to make serious decisions in such a small window of time. In most instances, many teens give in to the carefree nature they possess, which in turn leads to disappointment and, in some cases, regret.

How could someone with such criteria for a 'stable future' still succumb to a life that was all out of place? Some would attribute it to normal hiccups that we go through in our youth, and while this is true, I'd add it was even more daunting because I didn't know my purpose.

Defining Purpose

When you hear the words 'dating' and 'courting', there are very distinct thoughts that come to mind about each topic. For most, the term 'courting' is rarely used and has more of a sophisticated stigma attached to it. 'Dating' is often viewed casually, without a long-term commitment being directly insinuated. One seems to have a purpose that's clearly defined, while the other seems like a justification to say you'd like to keep this person around for a while. The objective here isn't to pit one against the other but rather to highlight that when something has a CLEAR purpose, we're more likely to treat it with intent. When you understand the purpose of something, you're more likely to commit to it.

Purpose is often coupled with career choice; courting is often associated with marriage. Both come with a stigma, and both seem to require a sort of permanence. You wouldn't say you're courting someone if they've shown no desire to commit to a 'forever' journey with you. So why do we associate our career choices with our purpose? It's as if the two are bound by life or that the same level of commitment is attached to both.

A career is something you choose, but a purpose is something that is given. There are no direct parallels. In fact, you can have one without the other. Purpose exists with or without a career. Whether I decide to become disciplined or I'm the laziest human on the planet, my purpose will still exist.

Purpose can be wasted, but it cannot be removed. It's as unique as your DNA, or your fingerprint. Purpose shapes your life more than a career does. A career affords you with an opportunity to gain more resources than you started with, but purpose takes the limitations off of life.

Purpose takes an individual who never should've been given a shot and gives them the opportunity to impact others even when they have more resources than he (she) does. Purpose is what we were designed to do. Career is, "What do I want to do?"

The purpose of war has a higher agenda than the battles that occur during a war. War is the cause for the fight, while a battle is the result of the fight. In a war, there are a series of missions that occur that have to be completed. A mission is meant to pass on after it's completed. Missions don't have permanence. Wars have the capacity to last for an individual's entire lifetime, but a mission has an expiration date.

Let's take, for instance, someone who's preached for forty years. After time, we notice things like a decrease in their attendance or a lack of congruency with current times. Maybe the congregation feels detached. Preaching is part of an assignment, and it comes with a time to end. It's not an endless task that one is to fulfill until the day they die.

Often, we mistake our gifts and assignments in life for our purpose when in reality, they are gifts to assist in completing whatever missions we've been given by God. God equips us with passion for a reason: so that as we chase after him while fulfilling his calling for our lives, we may be motivated and encouraged to complete his work.

God never leads you to a place where he won't provide. This is a crucial point because most of us try to compensate for our purpose by busying ourselves with a bunch of tasks that we feel help identify our purpose or what we were created to do. Purpose, in its simplest form, is obedience to Christ. Because this is a difficult concept for most to grasp, it leads to a lack of fulfillment of purpose in the lives of many.

Purpose fills the void we all seem to have and brings clarity to the complex parts of our life. In my own life, I've wrestled many times with being obedient to Christ, but each time I submitted to the leading of the Holy Spirit, I've seen the purpose of God fulfilled in my life.

How might one walk in obedience, you ask? Or the more frequently asked question, "How do I know when God is speaking to me?" One thing that we come to learn about God and his nature is that he is multi-faceted. Throughout the Bible, we witness many occurrences of God speaking to various individuals, sometimes audibly, sometimes through signs and wonders, or even through messengers (prophets, angels, priests, etc.). We see this in John 14:25-27, as Jesus tells his disciples that he will leave them with a helper.

> *I'm telling you these things while I'm still living with you. The friend, the Holy Spirit whom the Father will send at my request, will make everything plain to you. He will remind you of all the things I told you I'm leaving you well and whole. That's my parting gift to you. (MSG)*

Jesus signifies in this text that the Holy Spirit will be readily accessible to us and reside with us; and that he will make the instruction and wisdom of God plain to us. He even goes a step further to state that he will remind us of all the things Jesus told us. It's important to know that Christ is speaking not just present tense but future tense; and that as we walk with Christ, we can be reliant upon the power of the Holy Spirit to lead and guide us. He's God in spirit form, and he resides here with us. The Holy Spirit is always speaking, but because of our tendency to mystify his presence and relation to us, we assume it's an experience rather than a constant companion who resides here with us.

Christians tend to believe, "Something just told me to do it." This isn't limited to Christians either. Many non-Christians also have divine encounters where they feel something very significant was placed on their conscience. God is not just limited to our thoughts but frequently speaks through individuals, events, and feelings we just can't seem to shake.

One day, I was at a restaurant grabbing food with my wife, and a younger guy walked up to me and said, "What's your name?"

"Jaquan," I responded.

He stated, "Man, I see you surrounded by young people and young men. I see people being drawn to you and you having a gift to connect with people from all walks of life. I see you encouraging people and going into communities that most wouldn't feel welcome in and being able to really connect with individuals and to be a light to them."

My wife and I just turned to one another and smiled because, to this young man's surprise, I was pastoring youth and frequently talking with my wife about how I wanted more people to know that it's possible to live for God without feeling like you have to be imprisoned by the confines of religion and traditionalism.

On another occasion, January 21, 2020, after a period of fasting and prayer, I had a strong assurance that my wife and I would move to Dallas, Texas, by the end of that year. Exactly ten days later, Coronavirus had been declared as a global pandemic by our President. These were two polar opposite events that almost seemed to have two vastly different outcomes, but I was certain that we'd be moving.

To give more context, I'd just switched jobs at the time and hadn't even been employed at that company longer than two weeks. How was it possible that we'd move all the way from Minneapolis to Dallas with no job, no relatives, and no friends? It would just be my wife and me. We'd be leaving behind all we knew and all we had. Not to mention we were in the middle of a pandemic—how would it be safe to move or relocate anywhere?

Still, I couldn't shake this feeling. Each time I attempted to quiet my mind, I'd get another reminder. We'd be in conversation, and someone would randomly mention Dallas, or we'd be watching a television show, and there would be a scene about Dallas. It seemed the reminders were constant.

So, I said, "God, if this is your plan for us, please give me a sign."

The month of April came, and one day I felt the Holy Spirit leading me to talk to my boss. I was so nervous, but I couldn't ignore the instruction I felt God was giving me. I walked into my boss's office, and it couldn't have been a better time to catch her. She had no more calls for the day and no more meetings to attend. Nervously I approached her desk and asked if she had a few minutes to talk. Cheerfully she responded she was free to talk and invited me to have a seat. Quietly I collected my thoughts then began to inform her that my wife and I were thinking of moving.

Much to my surprise, she stated that she'd love to help. Immediately she asked the whereabouts of where we were thinking of moving. I stated Dallas, Texas. She gave me a chuckle and mentioned that Dallas was practically her second home because her best friend lived here. Not only did her best friend live in Dallas, but she worked for the same company we were employed by and might be willing to allow me to transfer to her specific location. It became apparent that none of this was coincidental: not only was I able to see that from my boss's response but also because company policy stated otherwise: employees could not be considered for a transfer (even internally) if they hadn't been on the job for a minimum of twelve months. In addition to that, you couldn't be promoted from your role if you had not performed in that role for at least a year (and I'd only been with them just shy of four months). Needless to say, there was a hiring freeze at our job during this time due to the pandemic and the uncertainty of further employment for those afflicted with the company. For three months, there were absolutely no job postings on the internal site.

Then one day, I happened to come across a posting in Irving, Texas, a city I'd never heard of. The role was a leadership role and required experience in auto financing, which I did not possess. After applying for the job, I was immediately screened and passed along to the recruiter. Surprisingly, after interviewing for the role, I was denied. The recruiter never reached back out, and I heard nothing for another six weeks. One day, I received a call from a Texas number: it was the hiring manager. She was apologetic for reaching out to me so late and proceeded to tell me that she was very upset to see that my application had not made it through. Not only was she upset, but she'd brought it up to her manager; and as a result, they offered me another interview.

After the interview, I didn't hear anything for another couple of weeks. Then one day, I noticed I had a missed voicemail. I played the message, and it was the same recruiter calling back to offer me the position in Texas! In that very moment, I thanked God.

There are no coincidences. This was a gentle reminder that purpose is directly connected to our obedience to Christ. How many times have we had a *something just told me to…*' moment? All too often, we don't realize just how many ways God tries to guide us toward our purpose daily.

Purpose is what brings you from hardship to success. It is what takes you from laziness to consistency. Discovering your purpose in life is like bringing light to darkness; sight to the blind; sound to the deaf. It's the missing link in the journey to success.

Now what does all this really mean, you may ask? I'd say

to you that when you have purpose in life, you have a better sense of direction. When you make decisions concerning your life, you'll become more aware of consequences, outcomes for your future, and the importance of the path you follow.

Purpose can bring clarity to someone who feels useless; someone who might be caught in the cycle of finding a job, working that job for money, and ultimately living just to make ends meet.

When you discover purpose, you enter a workplace and say to yourself, "How can I run this place?" or "I wonder how much money they make off of our labor?" I used to work for a movie theater, and I had a coworker who had been there for almost twenty years. She had only reached the title of supervisor, though. One day, she was attempting to inspire us (the rest of the crew in training), and she said, "One day, if you work just as hard as me, you can become a supervisor as well."

I thought to myself, "I won't be here long enough for that to happen." Listen, if it takes you over a decade to rise up in any company, no matter how well known or wealthy that company is, it is because you have not discovered your purpose.

Someone who doesn't know their purpose will be like my former supervisor. In her mind, she truly believed that the longer you commit yourself to doing the same repetitive thing, you will eventually move up. She saw moving up as a 'reward,' but promotion isn't a reward for someone who understands the potential they possess. Promotion should be confirmation for what you already know about yourself beforehand. If a job, or anything you find yourself working for, discovers that they can 'reward' you by giving you a title, then you have allowed them to undermine you. You have not truly defined your purpose in life. Individuals who have a strong sense of pride connected to the work they do for an organization are seeking validation in life. They have little to no confidence in the capabilities they possess to make their own dreams come true, to fulfill their own accomplishments. They are busy fulfilling someone else's demands for the comfort of payment and recognition.

If you are trying to fill a void in your life by seeking the approval of others, then take some time to identify your strengths. Ask yourself, "What do I do well?" When others think of you, what do you believe comes to mind regarding you? Are you known for doing a particular thing well? If so, how can you capitalize on this?

For example, if you're a very organized person, taking a job at a fast-food chain may cause you to limit your growth in this particular area, not because it's a fast-food restaurant, but because there's usually a certain set of guidelines that are in place to keep places like this functioning. They need to produce high quantities of product with or without focus on the labor force. Individuals who are very organized need something to organize. Problem solvers cannot exist without a problem to solve. If you, being an organized individual, took a position in fast food, it would completely contrast being employed at a childcare facility or in a clerical (administrative assistant) field where your given task would be to provide structure instead of being given structure. Both scenarios would require you to improve in an environment where the routine changes daily.

How Do I Navigate?

Purpose can be appointed, and it's a directive that one can give themselves. Although your purpose may feel that it's defined by your passion, it does not have to stay limited to just one specific area. Say, for instance, you're passionate about social justice; this does not mean the only option that you have in life is to become a social activist. In this situation, your purpose would be clear, which is to become a voice for the underserved (whatever group that you may feel requires more representation).

Frequently, we allow other's methodical ways to influence our purpose, and many have fallen victim to this tactic. Instead of filtering through options to fulfill our purpose, the reality of defining purpose comes to surface and it quickly becomes clear that we don't understand purpose. Furthermore, it is common that we don't know what purpose is, and more importantly, we don't have a clear understanding what our own personal purpose is in life.

To define purpose, we must visit a very conventional definition of what this is so that we can gain a clearer understanding of what this looks like. Merriam-Webster's dictionary defines purpose as 'The reason for which something is done or created; or for which something exists.' An example of this would be a parent training a toddler to eat with a spoon instead of their hand. A spoon has a clear purpose: it's a tool to assist with eating food. There's no logical way to eat cereal with milk without a spoon present. You wouldn't eat macaroni without a fork, and you wouldn't slurp juice off of the floor. It's evident that things with a clear source of purpose often help enhance what we have been presented with in life. Uber has committed themselves to the purpose of transporting people at a cost-efficient rate while providing that excessive individualized experience. In the same regard, Uber cannot exist without vehicles; and more importantly, without people.

When purpose is functioning in our lives, our goals can come to pass. The trick to understanding purpose is to see your end goal. For most, this can be where the struggle comes in, learning how to navigate through the turbulence of life and foreseeing an end goal. Many grow weary or discouraged as they pass through life's trials; and therefore, purpose becomes a bit 'cloudy.'

Most also assume that once they establish their purpose that no hardship will follow. Friend, I'm here to personally tell you that the moment you define your purpose, opposition may come to assault right away!

After one defines purpose, the next step is to develop a game plan or a strategy. Let's say your goal is to help prevent youth homelessness. Providing shelter is only one part of the strategy. One might have to consider developing a 24-hour assistance plan (for youths struggling with drug addictions or severe illnesses), hiring a reliable team of dedicated and dependable staff, gathering food, providing schooling and cognitive development programming, etc.

But this is just one facet of this dream. You see, defining purpose is one thing, but an effective strategy is the momentum behind the propeller. A goal CANNOT and WILL NOT come to pass without a game-plan. When people are motivated by purpose alone you see no results. These individuals are what I like to refer to as 'Purpose Politicians'—someone who will sell you a dream that will never come to pass or will delay seeing it come through. Now considering this example, I'd like to say that some 'Purpose Politicians' can't help themselves. They were sold a dream with no fulfillment and didn't learn to apply action to thought.

On the other hand, some 'Purpose Politicians' struggle with low drive or ambition and sort of give up when the leg work comes into play. To that individual thinking of ending youth homelessness, it may seem like a noble cause or noteworthy thing to do until the amount of effort it takes to complete such a task becomes visible.

When I first started my business, I decided that I wanted to bring spoken word across my city. I realized that this was an untapped market, particularly within the region of Minnesota. Initially, I was game to find a couple of open venues and just host my own 'open mics,' but this seemed to be an already up-and-coming popular event to do on college campuses around the twin cities. As I went to these open mics to perform as a local artist, I noticed that the star talent stood out from the rest who touched the stage. I also noticed the standing ovations quickly overshadowed the timid girl or boy who hit the stage reading quotes that even Socrates himself would've had a hard time comprehending. These recognizable individuals needed a platform to perform; they needed a space to be publicly displayed. It was clear they had talent, and I quickly decided that I would provide that space for them. So, I figured I'd book a spot on my college campus and invite people I was impressed with to come and perform.

I pondered this idea for a few days and then I felt it needed more. I sat on my couch, and created my strategy, or in more distinct terms, my 'vision.' I decided that this thing was bigger than just myself and that if I'd just done another open mic then, it'd be gone with the other fads that young adults so quickly forget. As soon as the next popular event surfaced around college campuses, open mics would become a thing of the past. I asked myself, "How can I define myself? How can I too become set apart from the rest?"

For many, purpose never quite fully becomes developed because, in order to 'know why something exists' (revisiting our earlier definition of purpose), we must understand its distinctive nature. As I continued to decipher the questions, my purpose became clearer and clearer. I was able to narrow down my intended audience while offering them an exclusive experience because I'd reviewed all that I could do for just this specific group.

Many times, our ambition drives us away from a clear and distinct goal. Our purpose can never become aligned due to complacency. Have you ever met an overly ambitious person? Someone who can never sit still? A person who's always telling you what their next endeavor is? That one friend who always has a new job when you meet them? People like this will never fulfill their purpose in life. Because they are so focused on all they want to do, they will never complete what they are able to do.

If you struggle with this way of life, understand that the best solution is to focus on what's within your reach. Otherwise, you'll be no different than a dog tied to a tree. People will hear you and think you're coming, but we'll never see you show up.

My parents often told me, "Worry about what you can control." My father would often follow up with, "I won't be losing any sleep over that." And as complex as these statements seemed to be when I heard them growing up, it's important to focus on what they both elicit. The main point was that you can't dedicate time to things that aren't directly related or pertaining to your life. If we remember nothing else, remember that purpose is connected to our lives; and if our lives don't align with our 'purpose,' then we must not worry about it. Like my parents would say, "Only worry about what you can control." In other words, those who take time to develop so many ambitions about multiple things, and don't find time to focus on one of these, only prove that they don't understand purpose or have a strategy to carry this out. Therefore, no goals can be accomplished.

Eventually, I developed a team to help bring forth the vision I had created. The four of us formed what later would be known as Poetic Mynds. More importantly, instead of following the trend of open mics, I was able to identify a need and meet it. As mentioned, the need was a space for talented up-and-coming artists to express themselves and to be recognized by the public sector, but for it also to be organic. In order for this to take place, I had to evaluate the interest of my clientele as well as myself. I recognized that all talented people could take stage, but it means more if you earn a spot on the stage. So, I established the idea for a casting call, to also approach certain talented individuals I had witnessed, and at the same time, open a window of opportunity for them to be able to invite others who they felt could enjoy the stage as well. This helped weed out any detractors, which you often face when trying to bring a dream to reality.

Change is constant and can't be stopped. Most people view change as a negative thing when, in reality, change is neither negative nor positive. It is an opportunity we all have to take advantage of. The way change affects our daily routine is what influences our perspective on whether this is a 'good change' or 'bad change.' Because so many of us fail to plan in life, we become apprehensive toward facing change. You see, there are two things in life we cannot control, one is time, and the second is change. Both are inevitable to escape, and the only defense we have against missing out on the benefits of both are to plan for the course of both possibilities.

Living In My Dream
But Not Making It Happen

While I was writing this book, I frequently found myself living in the daydream of my book being completed and how I would feel so 'accomplished', but the more I reveled in that opportunity, the more the process of writing became delayed. So much time was lost by focusing on the possibility of having a successful book finished that I never actually got around to completing the task at hand.

Many times, we find ourselves in the position of complacency because we focus more on all the benefits of a 'good change' instead of allowing this to happen in our life. Living in the realm of possibility prohibits the chance for 'reality.' It's become so acceptable to dream so big that we miss out on time and opportunity to advance our position in life. If we cannot stop change or time, then that means every moment in our lives is critical—no matter how big or small the situation seems.

What drives you in life? What propels you forward in harsh circumstances? For some, it is a moral compass, while for others it may be to leave a legacy for their lineage. For another group, it could be to prove to an adversary that they are capable. One thing we can all agree on is that no matter what your reasoning is for pursuing anything in life, the undeniable truth is the underlying factor is 'faith.' Nobody can complete any action in their life without the faith or belief that the action can be carried out.

Now faith is the substance of things hoped for, the evidence of things not seen. Hebrews 11:1 (KJV)

Being a man of faith, I tend to gravitate toward scripture for encouragement and personal instruction in my life. Since we all have a variety of things that we place faith in, what works for one individual may not be what propels another individual forward. Ultimately, it's inevitable to have faith in something while pushing through life. An atheist has faith that there is no higher authority, just like a Christian (believer) has faith that God is the navigator of their course of life.

Every individual needs a strong sense of faith to complete any action. In the scriptural reference, two particular words stand out of great significance. The first is 'substance' and the second is 'evidence.' Substance refers to something tangible, possible, or within reach. Faith makes hope tangible or a reality for those believing for whatever they are seeking to come to pass. Secondly, the word 'evidence' means a sign of something or an indication that there is existence of more to a particular thing. Faith will lead us to hope for greater and believe for better. As a result of this, we come to a place of acceptance that what we are hoping for exists.

Counterfeit

We're taught to dream big and not repeat the mistakes of our past. These two pieces of advice truly shape the line of thinking that we embrace the rest of our lives. Most people hear these sorts of statements and believe it's encouragement when actually it's a cage you place yourself in, mentally confining you. When we are constantly in pursuit of erasing our past, we slip into comparison, which leads us to timidity. One thing that anyone operating in purpose cannot do is be timid. Embracing the calling and purpose that God has appointed you to causes you to embody a boldness and confidence in his gifting. When we operate at a high capacity in our gifting, that's referred to as God's anointing. If we are not careful, we can accept counterfeits of purpose. Naturally, counterfeits can be hard to spot because they may have all the makeup of the real source. They look promising and even seem to may carry a righteous cause, but they can still derail you from the plan that God has for your life.

This is why we must be so careful to evaluate our passions and see if this thing I'm so 'committed' to is something that God is even calling me to focus on. We have the capacity to awaken things prematurely. Because we are created to be 'creative,' we don't understand the severity of submitting ALL of our plans to the Lord. We were fashioned in a way that only God can understand our engineering. This isn't to say that we can't predict habits of humans or even make inferences about how we think or speak. Ultimately, it's to highlight the fact that if we can't even fully comprehend the goodness of God, how much less are we able to comprehend the potential we have to passionately pursue a desire that we aren't called to.

Temptations have a stigma of only being negative, but the truth of the matter is temptations are just strong desires to pursue things that our mind and our heart suggest to us. They are not always malicious, but they are always self-seeking.

I remember early in my marriage, I was truly driven to be the 'provider,' as most husbands are. I wanted to replace the salaries of both my wife and I, which meant I'd have to look for a position that included a higher salary. At the time, I was working for a very prominent financial firm, and even to say I worked for that firm gave me a false sense of security. I was only twenty-four. A majority of my peers were still looking for work, let along finding a place that could offer them some form of elite status. While working at this firm, I happened to cross paths with one of the Vice Presidents one day, and during lunch, he asked me about becoming a financial advisor. I contemplated it, but ultimately, I decided I wasn't interested in the uncertainties that came with a full-time commission pay so early in my marital journey. I let him know that it just wasn't the time in my life where I could commit to something like that. He seemed really receptive to what I shared and encouraged me to put my family first.

A week or so later, he requested another meeting with me. As we sat in his office, he notified me that someone with my skillset needed to be in a position to lead a team. He gave me insight about what the structure was for the advisors at our firm. He even went a step further by saying, "Jaquan, if you can commit just a year of your time to this, I know you can do excellent!"

Apparently, I would be guaranteed a substantial salary for the first three years and within this time I'd need to develop a book of business and follow other business metrics that they'd developed for all those coming into this rigorous program. It all sounded so 'promising.' I went home and mentioned all of this to my wife. She simply asked, "Do you think you can do this?"

I reassured her I could. Truthfully, I was more than capable of meeting all of the prerequisites, but each time it was time for me to take my exam for certification I failed; it wasn't the appropriate timing. After we'd just planned and executed our own wedding, trying to find out where we'd be living, how our schedules would align, how we'd pay for all our expenses, etc.

Still, in the midst of all that chaos, it seemed so plausible and like a solution to calm the storm in our lives of bringing more stability by choosing this new job. It made sense and looked like a great opportunity, especially one that I could maintain. Isn't this what a counterfeit is? Something that has all the promising appeal of a potential solution to our 'right now' problem? It may even look like an answered prayer for most. Counterfeits are not meant to be obvious, but they are designed to appeal to our interest so that you may settle for less. This is why street vendors never go out of business because some people just don't see the value in purchasing the 'real' thing. The same way that so many of us are cheated out of purpose: we were not willing enough to put in the effort for the real thing. God calls us to 'live in the tension.' Most times, we can forfeit our blessing for the urgency of a now fix. We idolize the idea of stability and become stagnant because we have an idea that life with God means we are to reach this status of structure where our problems are now called to come to a calm, when in fact it's the opposite.

> *I've told you all this so that trusting me, you will be unshakable and assured, deeply at peace. In this godless world you will continue to experience difficulties. But take heart! I've conquered the world. John 16:33 (MSG)*

If Jesus could instruct his disciples this way as he faced his timely death, how much more crucial is it for anyone choosing to follow Jesus in today's world? God is privy to human logic and our gripes with life which is why he assures us that our dependence can remain on him and not our idea of whatever security we are In search of.

Merit-Based Christians

It's so important to know that God's grace was given to us freely. In the most simplified way, this means we could never do any more or any less to earn God's love towards us. God will never see you as less of his child because you've made a mistake or as more of his child because you help thousands of people. God is 'just' and fully unwavering in his character; he is perfection. Doing more good in life will never make your purpose bigger or more important than someone else's. Our impact doesn't determine our purpose; it's simply a result of our commitment to fulfilling our purpose. God doesn't hear me anymore or any less whether I'm doing 'good' or not. God is not moved by our flawed imperfections. In fact, the 'good' we think we are doing may not even be righteous in his sight so we should abstain from the frame of thought that states, 'The more I do, the more I will receive from God.'

Oh, what a self-indulged perspective! Do you really think our God is that small-minded that his formula for life would be figured out on your account (even though he created you?). I'm not 'closer' to Christ when I decide 'I'm right' for him. God is always near us, whether we are failing or succeeding. He is not limited; so, anytime we associate behaviors with a reward or particular sets of speech with higher ranking, then we divide ourselves. Our need to systematize situations causes a roadblock on our path towards the fulfillment of God's purpose in our lives. When we live in these 'Christian spheres,' we set divides. Never forget that God has already accounted for the fact that we'll miss the mark (even when we aren't trying to), which is why he so freely offers us his grace in return. Grace is simply the 'ability to do' through God's empowerment.

We are not disqualified from relationship with God because of our mistakes and we don't forfeit our position in his eyes just because we miss the mark. This is a self-defeating lie that has consumed many of us for years. It's a thought that's actually 'anti' God. We are reconciled by Christ, meaning he has brought us back to him. Even when we FEEL far away, we are never to shun ourselves from our father.

One time, our daughter had to eat food she didn't really like, so she lied to us about trying to spit the food out. When we asked her why she lied, she admitted it was because she didn't want us to be 'more mad at her' (in the words of a nine-year-old). We responded, "Honey, the disappointment doesn't change our view of you nor our love for you."

Sometimes, because of our own views and the perspective we place on God, we see him through our guilt and insecurities, which are both rooted in fear. God has not given us a spirit of fear/timidity (lack of courage or confidence) but of a sound mind. Our heart posture before God must be vulnerable yet secure in who we are to him: his children. A parent's disappointment or even their anger doesn't remove the position that you hold in their life. So let us not discount ourselves from who God is to us just because of our own shame. This is not the mindset that will keep you focused on the purpose God has for you. In fact, it will prohibit you from fulfilling his purpose for you if you hide behind your fears.

Applying Faith

Purpose is so crucial. The more we neglect responding to the instruction God gives us, the more dangerous our lives can become. Time is the one thing God isn't confined to, but it's something we are subject to due to the reality of living in the earth. Time regulates our lives and dominates every aspect of daily life. Every minute we waste, we can't receive back.

There are so many subtle distractions that plague us on a consistent basis that it's almost undetectable how much time is taken from us in a day. The term theft means taking something from someone but without the use of force. Our time belongs to us, yet it's taken so often we don't even recognize it's being stolen. We must be aware that just as real as Jesus is, there is also a very real adversary, Satan, and his biggest tactic is distraction. The Bible tells us:

> The thief's purpose is to steal and kill and destroy. My purpose is to give them a rich and satisfying life. John 10:10 (NLT)

The enemy wants to steal your time, kill your purpose, and destroy your spirit. We look for Satan to attack us in such identifiable ways that we lack complete insight on where he actually does come after us. One thing to remember is that the devil never fights fair so we can't be so naive that we think we'll see him in just one circumstance. What a way to underestimate your adversary. He's a skilled opponent and maybe more patient than you ever imagined. He loves to bombard us with many things at once as to overwhelm us and smother out our hope in Christ. The enemy sets traps up for you over a period of time. He's able to succeed at this frequently because of our blind spots, one of our biggest being prayer!

We need to truly understand the power and importance of prayer. Satan appeals to your desires, things you're already tempted by. This is why it can be almost undetectable at times because most of the things we allow to consume our time are already things we're vested in. Naturally, we are selfish. It feels normal to put myself and my desires above the needs of those around me, especially when it comes to prioritizing Christ. When we wake up, the first thing we typically reach for is our phone. Maybe it starts out us as checking the time, but we see we missed a call or a text message, so we click on it to respond. Now we see we have a notification from Facebook or Instagram, and we want to check that. Harmlessly, you move from one task to the next, but the reality is that none of this involves the advancement of God's kingdom's agenda on the earth. No matter how connected social media keeps me with people, it doesn't deepen my relationship with Christ. No matter how much I testify on my platforms, it doesn't remove the heaviness from my heart. These are only tasks that God can fulfill.

But we are so filled up with habits that we have no room for wholeness. Habits are formed by whatever repeated desires we submit to. If every time I desire to be recognized, I look to validation from people, then I will submit the power that God has already given me to others, thus allowing people to meet my desire. God tells us that he would grant us the desires of our heart, but we have to take pleasure in believing his validation is what we need.

Take delight in the Lord, and he will give you your heart's desires. Psalm 37:4 (NLT)

To delight means to take great pleasure in something. Could you imagine if you spent time delighting in God? Ask yourself what that would consist of: would it be highlighting only the good things? The more you delight in God, the less you expect from him, but also your heart becomes compelled to serve him.

So much of our journey on earth can result in time wasted because of the well-schemed tactics of Satan. Time isn't something we treasure as much as we should. We highlight tasks and events we'd rather partake in, allowing the enemy to consume so much of our time. Remember, a plot is to be figured out, but because we are typically self-absorbed, we don't plan to prepare. This is what the Bible refers to in Hosea 4:6: *My people are being destroyed because they don't know me. (NLT)* We can live in ignorance when we choose to neglect getting to know the purpose of God for our lives.

Being accountable is recognizing what you don't know and seeking that information (just like you did with this book!). God wants us to gain understanding about his purpose for our life so that we can prepare for attacks against the enemy. The more we continue to pursue only what we desire, the more we become deceived into thinking there's no threat to our lives.

Our journey in life isn't about being in conflict with one another but waging war against Satan's army and his tactics. Everything that we do in this life is either our agreement with the will and purpose of God or in support of our accuser and his hope for us which is to perish (to end our life without knowing Christ). Have you ever tried to setup a surprise for someone? This isn't a task that requires just one skill. When planning a surprise, one must be attentive. You'll find yourself studying your subjects' wants, desires, and habits just to make sure whatever you are presenting them with is something you're certain they'll be drawn to. This is exactly how the devil approaches us: he studies our every move, observing our desires, our actions, the company we choose to keep, anything we do. He pays attention to us even more than we pay attention to ourselves. Then at a time of his choosing, he bombards us with suggestions and presents different obstacles before us that either appeal to our desires or impact our emotions. His objective is to keep us so caught up in self that we shift our focus from God.

You can't have FOMO (fear of missing out) and faith; The two don't correlate. There is no algorithm for life, we can't predict tragedies, and we can't avoid problems; at some point, they will occur. However, our perspective about life's interruptions has a significant impact on how we view our lives. One main reason social media is so successful is that it transports you to your own world, a reality that only exists in your mind. It is a portal that we go through in which nobody else can enter. Social media transports you to the best version of your biggest insecurities. If I'm someone who often feels neglected, I can channel attention to my virtual persona. I can give the illusion that I don't care about others' opinions or make my life look problem-free. I have all the advantages I need with the power of social media. It puts you in the driver's seat (though it keeps you in comparisons). The wonder of it all is that everyone feels they have the same level of independence in the world of social media. No person sees themselves as a replica. Nobody sees that, in one way or another, they are followinga constructed idea of what uniqueness is. I believe the more someone has a fear of missing out, the more they are led to be consumed with only their wants and desires. It's a perfect playground for the enemy to defeat you.

A life of comparison is a hard life to live because it keeps us bound. It keeps us limited and makes us feel smothered. The first step on the road to purpose is living life by faith. Our faith is important because faith activates purpose.

Faith is the trust that we give God to lead our lives and faith is constant. Nothing should eliminate our faith. Yes, our faith will be tested, but this for our development. James tells us:

> Consider it agreat joy, my brothers and sisters, whenever you experience various trials, because you know that the testing of your faith produces endurance. And let endurance have its full effect, so thatyou may be mature and complete, lacking nothing. James 1:2-4 (CSB)

Whenever we are faced with problems, it's natural to want that problem to go away. It's an inconvenience to our lives and whatever we were expecting, especially when we seem to have no more room for another problem to occur. Essentially, what God is

Jesus was God wrapped in flesh, yet he still had to decide to operate in his purpose. Nobody is above purpose because purpose involves obedience to God.

communicating to us through these moments of difficulty is to strengthen your trust in him. He reminds us that he's always by our side, that we can count on him. It can be difficult to remember this in crisis because crisis tells us we need a solution now! Our emotions are powerful. God gave us the gift of emotions so that we could experience life the same way he does. God feels, thinks, and decides—all the same characteristics he created us with. This is what he meant by creating us in his image and his likeness: we were given a soul.

Our soul is made up of our mind, will, and emotion. We were given great capacity as humans, and God wants us to learn how to navigate through life's journey with the tools he designed into our makeup. It's natural for us to exercise faith; we do it almost unconsciously. You never contemplate if a chair will hold you up, you just have a seat. You never make the mistake of thinking food won't satisfy hunger. You have faith that these things will fulfill the task they were intended to, and that's exactly how God wants us to trust him. Our faith should be so natural that we second guess nothing he's able to do. He reminds us in his word that he's able to do whatever he needs.

Now to him who is able to do above and beyond all that

we ask or think according to the power that works in us.
Ephesians 3:20 (CSB)

Isn't that something? God is able to do more than we ever imagined. He's without limitation! Why wouldn't you want to trust a source like this?

The moment we decide to trust God and exercise our faith is the very moment we begin the journey of identifying our purpose. Remember, no matter who you are, there is still a choice you have to make to operate in your purpose!

The Existence of What We Hope For Becomes Real

Any great leader or person of power will tell you that faith or believing in their cause (whether positive or negative), is what made it possible for them to reach their goal. For all intents and purposes, our humanness demands a certain level of belief in our ability to complete the goals we set for ourselves. I would attribute this to that silent pride we all have buried somewhere underneath our likable nature or positive character. It is an inescapable reality that all of us face the need to be validated for the way that we accomplish the tasks we set out to do. There is a void in us to be filled, and we often try to fill this with people, things, and temporary goals/vain ambitions.

A common misconception in today's world is that you must look 'The Part.' This way of thinking has infiltrated so many—almost everywhere you look, there is a focus of proving to others what we would like to be perceived as versus what we actually believe of ourselves. Social media is a culprit for so much of this kind of behavior. Whether it's 'relationship goals,' 'how to make $1,500 in just 24 hours', or 'how to start a successful online business,' we are drawn away by the appeal of looking and sounding the part. The processes of achieving any sort of notoriety doesn't entice us the same way.

So often we measure success by the number of tangible things we receive, but success is best determined by the level of responsibility one has. A Chief Executive Officer (CEO) isn't considered 'successful' because of the amount of money he has (although that's an obvious component). His success lies behind the responsibility attached to the title. As CEO, you're entrusted with the livelihood of the entire company as well as the employment of a larger body of labor. The salary of a CEO matches the level of responsibility attached to the role. You wouldn't pay a manager six figures because the level of responsibility doesn't match the hierarchy of job roles.

Today's societal standards are misguiding, and the nature of American culture misleads so many to believe that high standards are an indication of success. In reality, high standards are truly just a deceptive desire for people to meet expectations that they have not proven to be capable of executing. The manager at a Speedway gas station would presumably have much less responsibility than the office manager at a 3M office.

Speculation has a huge role to play in the construct and analysis of our job placements. If we assume that 3M as an entity has a more reputable image, we will seamlessly integrate our thinking towards the idea that anyone who joins such an organization deserves higher compensation. A business has full right to determine the set up for their pay structure, and obviously the more money a business is generating, the larger the opportunity it has to create higher pay brackets for the employees. However, a significant factor is the idea we have towards the overarching standards we believe define the value of jobs/roles. A lot of people focus on looking the part. Up-and-coming generations take this advice too literal.

You don't have a desire to help end a struggle without knowing how to fulfill the need.
-Jaquan Kline

Thinking is not a qualifier for your success, but action is the determining factor for the measure of our success. Success is relative but what is definitive is a record of successful decisions made. This doesn't make one exempt from failure; in fact, this probably makes one more susceptible to it, if only by focusing on making impactful decisions. The point here is that we cannot just have successful thoughts live in our minds and neglect the responsibility to act upon any of these thoughts. When we execute the thoughts of success we believe to have, the action of carrying out these thoughts leads to a series of other responses that ensure or neglect the validity of what we think.

If Bill Gates just thought all day long about how a computer could benefit from a strategic operating system that could clearly communicate commands and tasks for this machine to deliver for its user, then we would have never had the opportunity to experience this and determine whether these thoughts produced a successful product or not. Success is reinforced when whatever you bring to the table causes a reoccurrence of use; or acts as a permanent solution to a common problem. The magnitude of one's success is largely dictated by the level of solution or analysis they bring to an issue.

Suits Don't Signify Success

How do we implement 'action' behind our desires? Better yet, how do we know which of our 'ambitions' are healthy to pursue, and which ones we pass on? Often the approach we are taught to take in life is instructive (following instructions/orders). This mindset is so engrained into us that it's hard to decipher when we are applying this to a particular situation.

For instance, let's reference the statement, 'Follow your dreams.' How often is this a mitigating factor in avoiding pitfalls? How does this particular statement prepare you for opposition when those 'dreams' face obstacles or seem unlikely to come to pass? What is the criteria for deciding when to give up on a task? Many times, we are given formulas for how we must execute a task, and when the formula fails to produce the proper results, we do away with the subject as a whole. I think what we lack most is effective strategy. True guidelines provide a great framework in accomplishing a goal, but strategy enhances our ability to navigate through obstacles. How many hundreds of businesses never made it past their first year because of poor strategy? How many individuals have never recovered from bankruptcy for fear of failure? Strategy is the combination of endurance and resiliency. We are often so dependent on instruction that we lack our own intent. It's possible for everyone to accomplish their goal if they set the expectation according to their own standards.

My timeline for growth doesn't have to coincide with yours, but more importantly, we can't become discouraged when the insight we gain from others doesn't parallel with our expectations. It's common for self-help books and motivational speakers to persuade us into their perspective on how to execute plans of action from their own lives in order to achieve the grand success they've seen. This information is always packaged in a way that seems so accessible to your current situation.

More importantly, the sense of urgency to act upon what they are delivering is always pushed. We live in a 'right now' culture which sets the false expectancy that all we hope to achieve is readily available after we check off a few boxes. The more that individuals follow this schema, the more disdain they grow for the process of working towards their goals which ultimately encourages them to be lazy and unmotivated. It's crucial to grasp the concept of patience and to apply that to 'goal setting' with the realization that manifesting things is not meant to be instantaneous.

Self-manifestation is so attractive to audiences and the ties that this has to the motivation world is so apparent. Everyone believes they can achieve instant notoriety and fame through mimicking these behaviors and repeating the same empty statements.

May he give you what your heart desires and fulfill your WHOLE purpose. Proverbs 20:4 (CSB)

God has designed us to desire what we are purposed to do; the challenge can be found in moving beyond what we allow to consume our minds. Sometimes being so focused on what we want can be the very reason that we are not fulfilling or able to identify our purpose. When we are disconnected or not in relationship with God, we aren't in a position of surrender to where God could touch our heart enough to reveal our true desires. We can be so set on what we want that we leave no room for God to impact us. It's often our passions we follow instead of our purpose. Passions can be well-intentioned things, but oftentimes they are merely ambitions without any substance.

When I was in my sophomore year of college, I felt so passionate about gatherings and community events. This all started because I attended a few open mics, and I noticed ways that they could be improved. I love to be in corporate settings or any form of large gatherings so naturally, this was a desire I favored. One of my natural traits is a facilitator: I was attracted to large gatherings and frequently offered my contributions.

The more I focused on the satisfaction and thrill that I experienced from attending gatherings of my peers and having some sort of influence on the structure of them, the more my desire grew stronger for this activity. It was all I wanted to focus my time, effort, and energy on. Thus, my passion began to develop to host and lead my own events. Within a few weeks, I'd written a business plan for how I could become an avenue for any aspiring artist or performer who wanted to have a space where they could showcase their talents and market themselves to various audiences. I began to attend other open mics within the city, eventually approaching a few other people and forming a collective called 'Poetic Mynds.' We set out to be a channel for any aspiring or local talent that wanted to display their abilities, network with peers, needed talent management, or any other resources we could offer.

What's interesting is this is how many of us operate in our lives. We find one thing to commit to that we like, and we divulge as much time as we can into that thing until it becomes a passion. Passions are simply a strong desire for something. Consequently, anything that we commit time to has influence on us. If I watch three straight episodes of a show, suddenly I have a desire to binge-watch. If I have more than one like on an Instagram post, suddenly I'm thinking, "How I can keep the momentum going with my future posts?" I spend one hour on the phone with someone I like, and suddenly I can't stop thinking about them. See, the thing with passions is that they don't take long to develop, but they quickly consume every part of us.

Nobody intends to become consumed with a passion but, because of our tendency to move towards self-sufficiency, we have an innate desire to become recognized for being perfect at whatever we do. There is a void that lives within us that can only be fulfilled by God since He satisfies us. We only come to know this through developing a relationship with Him. He is our manufacturer; therefore, He can anticipate and recognize every need, passion, and delight we have. It takes great faith to develop a true dependence on God, especially if we apply logic to our circumstances.

Passions are not negative and, truthfully, God gave us the capacity for passions because He intended for us to focus them on Him.

However, the more we move towards exerting faith, the more faith becomes our reality for life as we know it. This is crucial because when one is in pursuit of purpose, they must have an element of faith. Purpose isn't how well we can dream but how well we respond to instruction. We confuse our passions with our lifelong goals. So often we assume that if we feel strongly about something, then it must be what we were meant to do!

How To Identify Purpose?

When we are in relationship, we seem to thrive in ways we only remained stagnant in before. We become challenged to mature. This happens in many ways whether it be by circumstance or by communicating.

Communication is the most effective way of growing in any relationship. It's not a one-time action but rather constant. It's the pulse of every connection. Without communication, a relationship can and will deteriorate. As we journey through purpose, we become more aware of our purpose through communication with God. This happens through intentional devotion to him and when we pray. Prayer is meant to challenge whatever you are feeling and to put the focus on God still. Prayer helps you become at peace with what you can't control. This state of peace doesn't make sense to our natural mind or even align with our emotions, but it's the acceptance of our circumstances. When you rest in God's peace, you literally protect your mental state and manage your feelings. When we are told to pray, it can seem monotonous and even ineffective. Prayer is often widely suggested but rarely understood. The action of prayer is a listing of promptings that we should adhere to.

Praise, Repent, Ask, Yield

You see, prayer is how we strengthen our relationship with God. It's our daily communication, and when we approach prayer from this perspective, it alleviates the pressure of being perfect. Often, we feel that we should hide behind shame, guilt, or even our failures in prayer, when actually the heart of prayer is to relieve you of whatever has been burdening you.

When you speak to someone or confide in them, you're vulnerable because of the trust that you've extended. It will always be impossible to connect with a God that we don't trust. Believing in God has entirely nothing to do with trusting in God. This was a lesson learned in my marriage early on. My wife's first profession before founding her non-profit was a cosmetologist. This meant that not only she did she come with an extensive amount of knowledge about skin, health, and beauty, but she also had a knowledge about things like men's grooming techniques. Often, she'd see habits that I'd developed that were actually harming my skin and hair more than it helped, and she'd say something. At first, my responses were so subtle that I had no inclination that it was a lack of trust I had in her knowledge and ability to lead me in a new direction that would improve my poor habits. She'd say, "Hey honey, that's not good for your hair," or "Honey, that shampoo is actually damaging for the texture of your hair." And I'd respond, "Okay," or just quietly dismiss it, although, sometimes in my arrogance, I would even try to justify myself.

You see, I knew my wife was a trained cosmetologist and an expert. I'd even witnessed her perform many services on a wide array of clientele, not to mention she was employed at a pretty prestigious establishment. Many notable and prominent figures would come to seek the high-level services that were offered at her salon. I'd seen time and time again that my wife was trustworthy, but still failed to extend my trust to her.

Isn't this how we interact with God? We believe that he exists and that he's all powerful, all-knowing, even all-seeing. Yet, time and time again, we fail to trust him. He sees us leaning in a particular direction that could be harmful for us and maybe he carefully nudges us with a thought that won't go away. Sometimes he may even go a step further where he directly communicates to us through a close friend, spouse, or confidant that something is harmful, damaging or even unhealthy. Repeatedly we can be so casual with God that we respond in many of the same ways I responded to my wife, where we tune out his promptings because it doesn't feed our ego or doesn't sound like the advice we were hoping to hear. Why is that? Could it be because trust requires an element of not knowing? A level of uncertainty that can be difficult for any independent human being to endure?

Another translation for trust is faith. When we exercise faith, we actively believe that God will respond to us. You cannot pray effectively without an element of faith. Sometimes our faith may feel big and other times small, but the only requirement is faith, period. God says if we can display even the faintest of faith, he can utilize that.

> Because you're not yet taking God seriously,' said Jesus. 'The simple truth is that if you had a mere kernel of faith, a poppy seed, say, you would tell this mountain, 'Move!' and it would move. There is nothing you wouldn't be able to tackle. Matthew 17:20 (MSG)

I love the clarity of this version: Jesus is talking to his closest companions. Day in and day out, they did life together. Lived life right next to one another and even saw each other at their most vulnerable moments. They walked and talked with Jesus, witnessing mind-blowing miracles, yet they themselves struggled with fully trusting God. This shows you no one is exempt from lacking trust.

Trust is constant; it's not situational. Doubting is not trust; it's questioning the possibility of something. Trust is taking the risk to believe no matter what.

Plainly, we see Jesus tell his disciples that they were not taking God seriously, and this is because they weren't. Here it is, they had complete assurance that they could trust in God, but because of their familiarity, faith in self, and submission to their doubts, they didn't trust that their God would empower them even in the face of adversity.

Praise

The thing about trusting God is that is requires a heart check. Our motives with God must be pure because it leads us to a state of surrender where we can truly trust God. He responds to our faith, and if we don't have it, our relationship can coast and bear little to no fruit. When we pray, we must make it our goal to have a heart of *praise*. This doesn't mean that our problems don't exist; rather it shows God my motives are pure, and our relationship isn't based on a give-or-take basis. When I have a heart of praise, I have a heart of gratefulness; and out of this, a deep reverence and appreciation will humble us.

Repent

Repenting to God comes naturally when we are in this state of mind because we realize how undeserving we are for the many things he does for us. Repentance is not just being sorrowful, but it is being sincere with God. It's saying to oneself, "What did I allow to separate me from God in crisis?" Out of a repentant heart, we are led to ask God or make requests from him. Not for our own personal advancement but out of our lack in our humanity.

Ask

We *ask* God for grace in areas where we are in need or shortage. One might be led to ask God for provision for a family member because they are physically unable to intervene, or one might ask for a heart of humility for their constant battle with anger. Someone might even be compelled to ask God for insight on which decision they should make in a particularly difficult situation. God hears our concerns; we realize how limited we are, and we go to God due to our trust and love for him as our provider.

Yield

Naturally, we can expect answers to our requests almost instantly, and this requires us to *yield*. When we yield, we communicate to God that this act of prayer was a moment we come to God in our relationship and communicate to him the intimacies of our souls. God loves this heart posture and will respond to us every time if we take this pure approach before him.

It's funny that we tell others to pray but don't make it practical enough for them to follow. Prayer is our lifeline with Christ as it is the only way we can surrender whatever we are feeling bound by. Prayer is an outpouring of our thoughts and emotions that we trust God with as we run to confide in him. Sometimes praying may come from a sorrowful heart, while other times it may come from a joyful one. Either way, it contributes to the same level of growth and intimacy.

Paul reminds us about the importance of prayer in Philippians.

> *Don't fret or worry. Instead of worrying, pray. Let petitions and praises shape your worries into prayers, letting God know your concerns. Before you know it, a sense of God's wholeness, everything coming together for good, will come and settle you down. It's wonderful what happens when Christ displaces worry at the center of your life. Philippians 4: 6 (MSG)*

Here we see it emphasized once more the importance of prayer. We learn that prayer is not just an act but a series of things that we should incorporate into our daily life. Prayer should be habitual. It should be constant, and we shouldn't just treat it as an event.

Paul highlights that the continued benefit of prayer is freedom from the things that plague us mentally on a daily basis, such as worries. Every day we are presented with something to worry about, where we have to decide if we will respond out of our will; or submit to God's will. This is a crucial task as we cannot fulfill or highlight purpose on our own, but it becomes clear through submission to Christ day after day as we gain revelation through fellowship and grow in wisdom through our obedience.

Purpose vs. Meaning

How are you associating your purpose? Purpose is most often mistaken for meaning or the value behind why we do something. Although there is value to this line of thinking, it's important to note that purpose is much more than just our reason why. Purpose is guided by obedience and our ability to respond to instruction.

A lot of times, people want their work to have meaning, or they expect a sense of satisfaction to come about from pursuing a particular career. Firefighters feel more valued when they can rescue victims from life-threatening situations. Teachers are happy when they see students flourish under their guidance, and a lawyer may feel the excitement of winning a big case. The average individual would believe that the people in these scenarios have found their purpose in life. The truth is they may not have. The only thing each person in the examples I've given shares is a sense of satisfaction or accomplishment for completing a difficult task.

Western culture teaches us growing up that we should be recognized when we do a 'good' thing. Although this has served as one of the most undefeated methods for motivating people, it is a very flawed principle. It can be identified in every area of society. If I never get in an accident, my insurance company will offer me lower rates. If I utilize only 30% of my credit limit and pay on time, my credit score will eventually skyrocket. If I eat a balanced healthy diet, I'll maintain a weight and physique that I'm completely satisfied with. Yes, all these things bring about positive results, but none identify your purpose. What occurs so frequently is the continual pursuit of a life filled with needing constant satisfaction or a sense of meaning for what we are committing our time and energy towards. A millionaire could give someone a 12-step guide to acquiring millions in twelve months but that doesn't mean that after following these disciplines, they will have a newfound purpose. It just means that he is looking for gratification within his life whether it be internal or external.

Meaningful work can be accompanied by purpose, but the two are not associated; one is fixated on the need for approval while the other is rooted in a sound sense of who we are and why we have been placed on earth. For example, Jesus's purpose, I believe, was to be the Savior of our world. Yet He was also a carpenter. We don't get to hear an account of the joy He experienced in the moments He worked with His hands, but it is inevitable that He too had moments just like that.

Michael Jordan was arguably the greatest athlete on the planet at one time, at the top of his profession, but his purpose was not solely just to play basketball. We see that during his period of retirement when he played baseball.

We can become so consumed with the thrill of completing challenges that it obscures our view of the bigger picture. Whether that may be being able to inspire an entire generation to pursue entrepreneurial endeavors or building a treehouse for your neighbor's child, purpose impacts not only our lives but the lives of others. Purpose says, "You are valuable because…" It's followed through with action. Being the best at something is an inward feeling of gratification accompanied by admiration from others for a brief time if you keep doing that thing well. In the moment of failure, it all dissolves.

Purpose contributes to a legacy and teaches beyond what words can convey. Ecclesiastes 4:13-16 zeroes in on the plight of success or the version of success that we have been told to pursue by society. Success lasts but a moment; it is temporary. After you complete or succeed at something, you find another thing to be driven by. The team that wins the Super Bowl is only considered the most successful team of THAT year, not of all time. No matter how many times they win, they still have to prove it again!

> *Things and accomplishments will not fulfill you, titles, wealth, riches are all meaningless and are misleading to us. they offer a form of pleasure but it's situational. Ecclesiastes 5:10 (NLT)*

We have to remember that purpose is NOT a destination—you never arrive at purpose. It is ongoing, a walk, not an achievement or a stage that you reach. Purpose will always be in motion because it is connected to our calling. God has a plan, and you have a purpose, the two are synonymous. We cannot equate things like leadership and visible gifting to the fulfillment of one's purpose. God makes himself clear that we have plans of our own, but his plans prevail, and those plans lead to the fulfillment of our purpose.

What Does God Say About Purpose?

Ecclesiastes 5:18-20 highlights the principle that God has provided enough fulfillment in life alone, and the more that we re-center our focus, the more we can truthfully attest to this. Here the writer states:

> *Here is what I have seen to be good: It is appropriate to eat, drink, and experience good in all the labor one does under the sun during the few days of his life God has given him, because that is his reward. Furthermore, everyone to whom God has given riches and wealth, he has also allowed him to enjoy them, take his reward, and rejoice in his labor. This is a gift of God, for he does not often consider the days of his life because God keeps him occupied with the joy of his heart. (MSG)*

It's our innate tendency to fantasize about our aspirations in life more than we should. God designed us and this world for us to enjoy it. However, the reality is that our intentions have drastically changed due to the nature of our fickle human heart. We dream about fulfillment of all sorts and while this is not negative, it can mislead us into following our own path. God not only designed you carefully, but he intended for you to find reminders of his purpose for you even in the daily luxuries of life. Don't become so consumed with tasks that you fail to realize the countless reminders of purpose around you.

The Lord has prepared everything for his purpose. Proverbs 16:4 (CSB)

The first step in understanding purpose is to know that it's something that God has already worked within us. We are all PREPARED; God has intentions for all of us. Prepared means 'made ready for use.' When you purchase a cup, you don't have to determine its use because it's clear: it's a container for liquids. In the same way, when we view ourselves the way that we were conditioned, we begin to realize that we were designed as an answer to something or a solution to a problem in this world. God makes it apparent when He stated that we are prepared for His purpose. We see this more closely as we reference scripture: God's purpose was always carried out through His creation. It was not just limited to humans, but all things were created for God's purposes: trees, nature, animals, countryside, land, etc.

From the very beginning, we were created with intent and purpose. When we see down to our very makeup, we see that God intended to create a being that was made in His likeness (humans). Through humans, we see a reflection of the variety of who God is, the culmination of male and female. Just as God is Father, Son, and Spirit, each being is distinctly different. Each are completely whole in who they are and share some of the same attributes.

This is the same case for male and female: each possesses a mind, a body, and a spirit, yet they are uniquely different. This is the very essence of who God is: He is our Creator, our Comforter, and our Guide. However, He is still very much Jesus in flesh form, the Holy Spirit in spirit form, and our Father whom we depend on and look to for help.

> *Then God said, 'Let us make man in our image, according to our likeness.' Genesis 1:26 (CSB)*

Who is 'our'? Remember, God is three parts. We can conclude that this conversation took place between God the Father, God the Son, and God the Spirit.

> *So God created man in his own image; he created him in the image of God; he created them male and female. Genesis 1:27 (CSB)*

Pay close attention to how God clearly states our purpose the moment He created us: to be a mirror of His image while here on the earth. We are image-bearers of Christ, meaning we are like God. In His likeness, we are communal beings. Humans experience community through family, friendships, personal relationships, and various other communities (school, sports, jobs, etc.). God also made it a point to give us very distinct qualities that He possesses for us to fulfill purpose. He gave us the ability to think, have emotions, and most importantly, to choose our 'will.' These characteristics are important as we navigate through our lives.

We will need to exercise every one of these abilities in order to complete our purpose. Jesus would not have made it to the cross had He not thought that this was pleasing to the Father. He believed and felt that this was part of His assignment. He chose to do our God's will above His own. It was through each one of these attributes that we see God's predestined purpose for Jesus was fulfilled. He became the Savior of the world through submitting every part of Himself towards identifying with God's purpose.

This didn't mean that he wasn't permitted to fulfill other desires He may have had while here on earth. It just means that regardless of what He might have had a passion for, He never neglected His purpose.

How easily do we get discouraged when what we started off loving we end up resenting because it didn't turn out the way we envisioned? This line of thinking is what so often deters people away from fulfilling their purpose. The sense of satisfaction they are hoping to receive either dies out or disappears when they lose interest in that particular thing. Purpose has nothing to do with what we want but what God desires for us. When we surrender our preferences to God, it is much easier to adapt to His plan for our lives. He doesn't give us anything that isn't good for us anyway.

It's like feeding an infant. Sometimes infants spit out foods that don't taste as appealing to them, but it's still good for them. Parents generally act in the best interest of their children and will not give them anything that would harm them. Neither will they make decisions for them that will have unfavorable outcomes. When we 'think,' we apply reasoning to whatever we partake in or choose to do. We are not solely instinctive, like a fish or a bird. We are creative and designed to create something from nothing (just as God does). Because of these things, we have value to God, and we are made for God.

God works through all aspects:

> *We know that all things work together for the good of those who love God, who are called according to his purpose. For those he foreknew he also predestined to be conformed to the image of his Son, so that he would be the firstborn among many brothers and sisters. Romans 8:28–29 (CSB)*

These verses outline who we are and how the fulfillment of our purpose takes place. The framework suggests to its reader that being in relationship with God and LOVING Him is what allows us to see the fulfillment of His purpose in one's life. It even goes further by saying that God is so intentional that when we are in relationship with Him, our purpose comes to pass. We were created with intent enough that our purpose comes to life through connection with Him since He 'predestined 'us.

Being predestined is equivalent to being groomed for a profession well before you start. How can one fail this way? This is not to insinuate that one may not be capable of making a mistake while on this path, but it gives you reassurance that even when you fail, you still have purpose. Society says if you don't soar right away then you're not capable of success. Being a 'natural' at something never guarantees an obstacle-free journey.

Life is perilous and even bleak at times, but purpose is never subject to what we are feeling. Our emotions are not tied to our purpose. As humans, we tend to be led by our morale or inward compass (intuition), but this frequently leads us astray. While it may serve a purpose when it comes to having integrity and choosing the right company to keep, it has absolutely nothing to do with our purpose. Our will or emotion may lead us to be nice to someone if we are having a good or an exciting day, but purpose must be fulfilled regardless of our emotions. What emotion can do at times is motivate us to move closer towards our purpose—by rendering our will to do something we don't want to do when we are bombarded with the heaviness of life. Purpose is to be fulfilled regardless of your level of enthusiasm towards it. Jesus was not 'thrilled' to sacrifice Himself upon the cross, yet He still fulfilled that purpose. He accomplished it, as grievous as it was. Michael Jordan could barely focus during his 'flu game' in 1997, yet he willed himself to suit up in pursuit of his sixth title.

> *Purpose says regardless of what was, this shall be; regardless of what I feel, I still will myself to be.*

> *For God loved the world in this way: He gave his one and only Son, so that everyone who believes in him will not perish but have eternal life. John 3:16 (CSB)*

Although this is possibly the most quoted scripture to date, it clearly outlines God's purpose for humanity which was to provide the biggest display of love known to mankind. He did this despite the tumultuous relationship He had with humans (from Adam and Eve until today). Purpose is the navigator to our lives. It will not compromise itself for any extenuating circumstances and is never persuaded. Purpose has undying integrity, a commitment to accomplishing whatever it set out to do.

The interesting thing is that purpose is so clear if you don't fulfill it, another will come behind you to accomplish that thing. Moses' purpose was to bring the children of Israel to the Promised Land, but when he failed, Joshua fulfilled this purpose. Jonah hesitated to deliver his message to the people of Nineveh, and God sent Nahum to give not only the same level of detail but even greater clarity to the purpose He had for them. Purpose is neither 'good' nor 'bad,' it is simply an order that must be carried out, a predestined plan that must be fulfilled. God allows us to have an opportunity to follow His will and to align ourselves with His will. However, it's crucial to understand that this will be accomplished with or without you. It is His hope though that you would willingly participate so you may reap the benefit of obedience as well as the growth of character that we may need.

> *I cry out to God Most High, to God who fulfills his purpose for me. Psalm 57:2 (NLT)*

God has already created our lives with purpose, and that purpose has been predestined. We must live it out. The only way to do that is through real intimacy with Christ; forming a relationship and developing a connection where you are communicating with God and learning

His voice. We can do this in many ways, such as reading the Bible, praying, and meditating on the given principles. One might even consider becoming a part of a community of like-minded individuals. This will influence you to be more inward focused in your day-to-day endeavors.

Godly community is essential. Religious behaviors or traditional church culture passes as behaviors of 'Godly' people, but it's so important that we distinguish between the two. The type of community Jesus encourages us to keep is that which holds us to a standard of accountability. For a Christian, the great news is that the Bible has already set the standard. We don't have to focus on telling others what to do. Through our observations of how those we are in community with choose to conduct themselves, we can decide when it may be appropriate to inquire about things that may raise a concern.

For instance, say that I go out for a drink with friends, and I get very drunk. Someone in my circle of accountability may have a concern. Instead of preaching to me and damming me to hell, it would be more appropriate to see how my personal life is going. Our outward behaviors are indications of inward problems. There's something about human connection that gives us a greater sense of accountability.

Can two people walk together without agreeing on the direction. Amos 3:3 (NLT)

Godly community deepens our desire for an upright

walk in life. When you know you're connected with people who will call you out on a mistake or remind you when you are being the opposite of who you profess to be, there is a deeper commitment you feel to following a standard. When an individual understands that their excuses are no longer acceptable, this does one of two things: pushes them directly toward their purpose by making them realize they are failing on their own; or pushing them to choose to be driven by their own faint sense of accomplishment. I have seen time and time again that those who surround themselves in these types of communities thrive. They may encounter hardships and other difficulties, but they are more prone to resiliency. The troubles of life don't feel as heavy when your cohorts are there to remind you that you are free from being shamed when you don't meet the mark. They let you know you don't stop pressing toward the standard, but you will change over time—not instantly.

It's an equally great reminder in these situations to know that we manufacture all our own plans to succeed, but they don't always pan out how we anticipated. Mainly because when we're growing, our desires naturally change.

When I was sixteen, my only desire was to go to college and become a lawyer. That was my only plan, my only goal. But once I reached the collegiate level, I learned that there were so many other opportunities beyond just this one idea that I had been so focused on. I felt enlightened but also behind.

This is like how many people feel traveling down the road

of life. It's a familiar road. Many become accustomed to one particular way to walk that they feel out of place when life plants an obstacle right before them. Preparation isn't always the job of the one following, but it is for the guide. Remember, God is our guide and has anticipated any possible challenges or trials we could face along the way. We are well equipped, and He will continually keep us through every test since we are on the path that HE leads. Whenever we leave His path for our path, we are at a loss.

Accepting Purpose

You can make many plans, but the Lord's purpose will prevail. Proverbs 19:21 (NLT)

The problem we face in life is that many of us try to make meaning out of it. This may sound bleak, but life doesn't have 'meaning' because it's a gift. Gifts don't have meaning, but they do have value. They have significance and they cause us to express gratitude. Similarly, we should look at life in the same way. God gave life to us as a gift. He told us the main objective in this life is to acknowledge a dependency on Him and to live in a state of gratitude.

One year, my wife and I were getting ready to celebrate my birthday. I just wanted to dress up and have dinner at a nice restaurant. The day was not going as planned, with most of it spent waiting on my wife (at least this is how I interpreted the situation, as most husbands do). At the time, I'd just lost my car, so I had to wait on my wife to pick me up. We lived in Minnesota, which meant the weather was horrible. It had snowed that week, and the high for that day was six degrees with a low of negative five. As one can imagine, it's difficult enough being subjected to such hostile weather conditions along with not being able to celebrate special occasions the way you'd hope. My wife picked me up about forty minutes later than the time we'd initially planned for, and she could see the agitation in my demeanor. I was unsure of what the plans even were for that night because I was so unhappy. My lovely wife continued to extend patience to me, and we eventually pulled up to the destination. After a few moments of me simmering in my frustration, we finally entered the restaurant and when we did, I was speechless. There before me was two tables of my closest friends and a few of my relatives. There were balloons and many other decorations. There was a beautiful cake, sparkling candles; and afterwards, a beautiful hotel room decorated from top to bottom with treats, presents, and so much more.

Isn't this how God is with us? When we look at life and all the inconveniences we have on a daily basis, we remain in anger and frustration longer than we hope. It drives us to look for meaning in other places, in people, and things. We figure, if we accomplish this goal or impress this person or attain this new possession, it will signify a sort of 'meaning.' Repeatedly, we prove ourselves wrong when all along God has given us something so big as a gift. We are too distracted to grasp it and to value it completely.

The extent my wife went to in order to accomplish all she'd given and done for me that night was so much larger than what I was feeling. It wasn't until I walked into the gift that I shifted my entire view of the night. To this very day, I still share how this was one of the best birthdays of my life.

Unfortunately, we allow tragedies to point us toward temporary recognition of what we are gifted with. Death causes us to reflect on the importance of life and to appreciate the time we have since, "You never know what you have until it's gone." What if we chose to appreciate life now? What if I constantly made the declaration to say, regardless of what I face I'm going to live in a state of gratitude? Gratitude doesn't say, "I have no worries, I have no struggles, I have all that I need." It proclaims that I'm surrounded by adversity and a host of things that I could complain about; however, I'm going to focus on what I can appreciate.

We can become so consumed with the idea of what we believe we want or whatever we believe will fill a void, we become deceived. We may even become disillusioned and think that we are missing something because of the absence of a fantasy.

The purpose we have in this life is to be grateful. We have been given a lot, and it could all so easily shift. Problems overwhelm us because we remain in what we are feeling. The reason God gifted us with emotions is to identify whatever concern we are experiencing and bring it to Him. A state of panic is a lifeless state of being. It's a state where you feel paralyzed, but you aren't. It's like being in a glass room thinking that you cannot escape, but you can.

When we are consumed with God, we find ourselves less in a stance of the pursuit of life but more in a posture of surrendering. We give all that we have to Him because we want to become so full of Him. Carrying out this approach to life makes such a significant difference. The more we focus on God and what we do for Him, the less we feel self-directed. Independence is so opposite of how we are to be in our lives. In fact, God highlights all throughout the Bible how weak we truly are and how we were even created to be dependent upon him.

My power is perfected in weakness. 2 Corinthians 12:9 (CSB)

Another translation states, *My power works best in weakness. (NLT).*

I'm not discouraging anyone from pursuing a goal or a dream, but I am pointing out that every journey is filled with intersections, moments where we gain newfound insight or receive new wisdom that gives us fresh perspective. Perhaps it is simply the natural wisdom we gain as we live life and allow it to influence a new line of thinking.

The purpose in a man's heart is like deep water, but a man of understanding will draw it out. Proverbs 20: 5 (ESV)

Purpose is not one piece of instruction but rather a series of plans that we follow (as we are spirit-led). We accomplish a bigger goal by rendering ourselves for God's use. How can we identify purpose? We need others around us to bring it out of us. This can be by fellowship, seeing a need in a community, beginning to learn what drives you as you commit yourself to others, or someone speaking life into you. This helps ignite a fire that drives your purpose.

How Does Purpose Come to Life?

Plans go wrong for lack of advice; many advisers bring success. Proverbs 15: 22 (NLT)

We need people and connection to others in order to see our purpose come to life.

Two people are better off than one, for they can help each other succeed. If one person falls, the other can reach out and help. But someone who falls alone is in real trouble. Ecclesiastes 4:9-10 (CSB)

Your own life can be challenging, and your perspective can be obscured if you are only self-reliant. However, others help shed light on new perspectives which contribute to the pursuit of purpose and, in some instances, the fulfillment of purpose. We need others around us in order to witness our purpose fulfilled. Jesus' disciples were able to attribute to the fulfillment of his purpose because he allowed them in close enough proximity to see his obedience to God.

Our biggest pitfall as humans can be our obsession with looking perfect. We would rather keep a distance between us and others because the closer we allow someone, the more access they have to our daily lives. But in order for purpose to be fulfilled, we have to be in relationship. Make no mistake, whatever God has called us to fulfill in this earth will require the involvement of people. As I mentioned previously. God is a communal God and often delegates an assignment to someone for the benefit of others. God has not purposed you for yourself but for the exclusivity of others.

You were exclusively made to be inclusive!

There is a difference between working for gratification and working in your purpose.

> *Whatever you do, work heartily, as for the Lord and not for men. Colossians 3:23 (CSB)*

> *The way of a fool is right in his own eyes, but a wise man listens to advice. Proverbs 12:15 (CSB)*

What makes us a person is our soul. Our soul is made up of our mind, will, and emotion. We think with our mind, choose with our will, and feel with our emotion. Since our soul is the entirety of our beings as humans, we have to maintain the right focus in order to see our purpose fulfilled.

We can easily forsake our purpose if one of the three parts of us becomes influenced negatively. If the will is compromised, it can be detrimental to surrendering to God. Our will is composed of our ability to choose. Choice feels so natural and is a part of our autonomy as a human. However, we submit our desire to choose unto God's desires for us. Through this exchange, God reveals His purpose for us.

Let's say you are a parent of a fifteen-year-old, and they just received their license ahead of an upcoming birthday. Maybe one day you are having a conversation, and you give them a choice to decide what they want to do for their birthday. Let's narrow down the choices a bit, their choice and yours. Their idea is to have a sweet sixteen and invite all their friends to celebrate with them. The other option is a surprise from you, but they have to wait to see what it is on their birthday. After a few moments of consideration, they must choose which option they'd prefer. All along, they're unaware of it, but the gift you'll be surprising them with is a brand-new Mercedes Benz. You want to respect their choice as an individual, so you allow them to choose which is best for them.

This is just how God is with us— He allows us to choose even when He knows the best option for us. God doesn't rule over us with an iron fist. He wants us to align our will with His. Sometimes we are in such a rush for what looks or sounds like a good idea in that moment that we spearhead straight into the first option without knowing which direction God truly wants us to go. Just like a good parent, God doesn't discourage us from choosing, but hopes that we desire to align our choices with His or come to Him for insight. God's insight is His purpose.

Why Do We Feel So Compelled To Find Our PURPOSE?

This is an age-old question. When we think about it, we

all feel compelled to complete something in life. This is because we were made to create since God made us in His image and His likeness. He made us with the capacity to create. There is a part of us that almost feels incomplete when we aren't working towards or for something. Many times, this process or feeling is described as 'finding your purpose.'

However, one must truly understand who God has called us to be in order to understand our purpose. Purpose is not a 'task;' rather it is the act of walking out obedience to God. It is responding to the leading of the Holy Spirit, implementing the practical principles taught to us in the Bible, and more importantly, prioritizing God's will in your life above your own.

This is easier said than done though. Detecting our 'will' can be difficult when we are not fully surrendered to God. We may be unaware of how selfish we are because of our passions. Passions drive you to feel connection to what you're pursuing, so frequently we find ourselves justifying our passions over our purpose. Purpose can be uncomfortable to fulfill, even daunting at times. It requires a level of sacrifice as well as an obedience that challenges reason.

What guides us to our purpose? For some, it may be the idea that we hold the key to our own destiny. For others, it could be their intuition; and, for another, it could be that they believed they manifested their purpose into existence. The common thread amongst these scenarios is an element of faith that must be garnered in order to see these things through. Although I don't personally subscribe to these forms of belief or even endorse them, I can acknowledge the validity of developing a strong sense of faith in something. We are faith-oriented beings. It's inevitable that we will believe in something at some point. We see it in everyday life, from the working class to the wealthy. The belief that hard work will pay off or that it's possible to make an honest living. Even those with criminal pasts have faith in whatever principles they stood by. Whether it's the mindset that, "If you harm me, I should harm you," "Take from the rich for the benefit of the poor," or "Oppress the oppressor," each situation requires individuals to identify with the perspective they believe in.

No matter our background, level of education, or socioeconomic standing, nobody can skip the first stage when fulfilling their purpose: having faith in a few very simple, yet crucial, principles. (Be sure to read the accompanying scriptures for various perspectives the Lord gives on purpose.)

1. Our purpose is predestined or established before we've even lived out our lives. The reason this principle is so key is because it allows our hearts to be more receptive to God's instruction: walking in obedience with God.

   Proverbs 16:4
   Romans 8:28-30
   Jeremiah 29:11

2. We have no purpose outside of God and will not fulfill purpose by following our own plans.

   Proverbs 21:5, 16:9, 15:22, 19:21, 3:5-6, 16:3
   James 4: 13–15
   Matthew 6:33- 34

3. Purpose may not always align with your WILL.

   Proverbs 19:21
   Proverbs 16:3

4. YOUR WILL is not YOUR PURPOSE. We see that Jesus, the Savior of the world, God in human form, did not even consult with His own plans and desires in one of the most conflicting moments of His life. He realized it was not about His WILL or His own plans, feelings, and desires. It was about fulfilling the purpose of God, which requires sacrificing what He desired. How do we know what He desires? Through the Bible and its' teachings, but more importantly through the leading and fellowship with the Holy Spirit since He is our Guide and Teacher on this earth.

   Proverbs 3: 5-6
   Psalm 37:5
   Jeremiah 9: 23
   Matthew 26:39

5. The Holy Spirit helps us fulfill purpose.

Romans 8: 26–27

Understanding these principles really provides a clearer scope of how to walk in your purpose, even if you don't fully understand it. The biggest misconception people have about purpose is that it's an attainable goal we reach before the end of our lives. The quicker we realize our purpose cannot be fulfilled until we accomplish all that God has sent us to do in our lifetime, the quicker we will no longer allow feelings of anxiety and stress to overwhelm us.

Feelings of worthlessness, of having no place in society, or not having anything to live for stem from not knowing what purpose is; still yet, what it even means in relation to our lives. Many times, we blame others, and our circumstances, for us not understanding our purpose and not really knowing what we're supposed to do with our lives. This is actually a form of deception. The Bible makes it very clear that we have the capacity to understand more. Frankly, we don't put in the work so that we can. Hosea 4:6 illustrates that God is in dialogue with Hosea and reveals that people aren't living unfulfilled lives because they are weak and incapable. They are not even aware enough to know the plans they should make in different seasons of their lives. They are disconnected from the instruction and wisdom of God. John 3:16 states that God loves us so much that He sent His Son as a sacrifice to atone for any wrong that we ever did, or may do, in our lifetime. This is so we don't have to focus on being perfect or feeling inadequate for our failures. He even encourages us by saying when we accept Him into our lives; we don't have to perish or live life without meaning or understanding. He wants to grant us a life filled with meaning and help us to fulfill our purpose.

Failure Is Essential

Time and time again, the Bible reassures us that our shortcoming, failures, and various tragedies do not signify our success or even define our purpose but that they are actually a part of the predestined purpose God specifically has for you (Romans 8:28). But if I'm following my purpose, why am I experiencing problems?

> *Consider it a great joy my brothers, and sisters, whenever you experience various trials, because you know what the testing of your faith produces endurance. And let endurance have its full effect, so that you may be mature and complete, lacking nothing. James 1:2-4 (CSB)*

How many times have you, or someone around you, prayed, "Lord, please reveal my purpose to me," or "Teach me my purpose, God"? Even if we never audibly uttered those words, I'm certain that we've all thought them at one point or another. In fact, after praying things like this, we often encounter some sort of obstacle. Most of the time, we can respond to these obstacles with contempt, feeling inconvenienced, or we are frustrated since we didn't associate obstacles with purpose. The two just don't seem synonymous.

Fulfilling God's purpose doesn't mean that you will be exempt from trials or problems of any kind. In fact, they are inevitable and sometimes, even given to us by God to help shape or renew our perspective in a particular area. Trials are not designed to discourage you but rather to produce endurance in you. We must remember we are all given particular missions to accomplish that contribute to the fulfillment of our purpose. In the army, you go through rigorous training to prepare you for whatever that mission may entail. Similarly, this is the same process we encounter on our journey in life. Sometimes, we are unaware of areas where we may need more growth, but God is always able to spot our shortcomings. He pushes us towards certain situations that could grow our endurance in a particular area.

Many times, we may hear the aforementioned Scripture referenced and we think of endurance as one act. Endurance is not limited to just one area. It's the ability to withstand. Withstanding is not just making it through a tough time, but asks, "How do you maneuver through difficulty? How is your attitude? What principles do you apply to finding a resolve to your circumstance?" God uses trials to mold us. Whatever blemish or spot we have overlooked, He identifies and stretches us to the point that makes us more malleable. We may face various trials within the same situation that contributes to our endurance. God is so phenomenal that He can take one trial and equip us with enough endurance to withstand back-to-back situations. We miss the benefit of gaining endurance when we look to find a way to escape the inconvenience of a problem or the pain that comes from a loss or failure. God uses the most unorthodox methods to teach us such simple lessons. Never does He punish or harm us. Although His provisions might include the unexpected, it's never anything that doesn't align with His will or the fulfillment of our whole purpose.

Purpose is not necessarily a definitive thing but a journey of obedience. Mission is a part of purpose. While fulfilling certain missions, we may even set goals on how to achieve a bigger vision. It's all a journey towards purpose.

Purpose includes FAILURES. Don't ever think you're exempt from mistakes just because you're responding to God's calling on your life. Moses killed a man on his journey towards leading a nation to freedom (Exodus 2:11-14). God recognizes our humanness and has introduced grace to account for our failures. Failing does not disqualify yourself from any further success even if you fail repeatedly.

A person's steps are established by the Lord, and he takes pleasure in his way. Though he falls, he will not be overwhelmed, because the Lord supports him with his hand. Psalm 37: 23–24 (CSB)

Passion

What do you do when you feel like God identified your purpose, but your plans fail, your business fails, or your great idea no longer seems good?

Passion is what fuels you to complete your mission. God designed us all with a certain level of drive for specific things. Therefore, at times, we may feel that we lack 'interest' or 'passion' about specific things. It's important to remember that passion doesn't always correlate with your purpose, but it is more tailored to your mission.

Purpose is about obedience and responding to a call, while passion is the drive to fix whatever problem may be preventing you from moving towards that calling. For example, as a Youth Pastor, I often feel passionate about helping youth see the value in their lives at a young age. So much so that I don't mind spending hours at a time with them answering any questions as well as sharing my knowledge and experience with them. However, this doesn't necessarily mean I'm fulfilling purpose every time I do this. God has given me this assignment to work diligently and passionately towards setting the stage for whatever He is looking to do in their lives. I'm just a vessel. By the time some of them pick up this book, I could be working in a different capacity in ministry. In this season of my life, God said to pastor youth. In another, He could say, "Go and work missions' trips." It's important that we aren't led by our passions. When we are, it may cause us to stay working in one area a lot longer than we are supposed to.

Have you ever met someone who's no longer teachable? Chances are they've been working in a certain capacity for so long that they feel they know all there is to know about that particular subject and no longer seem open to change. This can be a sign of expired passion. God could've likely sent them various signs that it was time to move on to another phase in their life, but they stayed so focused on the passion they had for doing a specific line of work that they've gotten too familiar with their mission.

If I deliver packages for UPS and get the same route every day for five years, chances are I'm going to familiarize myself with certain things. Perhaps I'll get to know certain people in the neighborhood, memorize the route, or even decide the best time to arrive at each home for delivery. All of these things are good to be aware of, but each contributes to me gradually exchanging my passion for comfort. It can be difficult to detect the difference because both feel 'good,' both communicate, "I really care about a certain level of things, and I care that each of these things is done in a specific way." There are times some have familiarized themselves so much with what God called them to complete that the particular thing became their distraction. They couldn't move past it. Let's take David for example. He was so familiar with one aspect of his rule as king and being a fierce warrior. He gradually shifted his focus from purity and walking in holiness. This is what led him to eventually stealing Uriah's wife and having him killed in battle (2 Samuel 11). Is it possible that we sometimes get so accustomed to the comfort of our mission that we begin to lose our passion for completion?

Mission

Yes, we all acknowledge that David was a man after God's own heart but that doesn't excuse the lack of execution for that mission. We serve a forgiving God who loves us through every mistake and any failure, yet we are still capable of seeing whatever mission He calls us to fulfill to completion. There are many examples of this. Two of my favorites are John the Baptist and Paul. Both were required to fulfill a mission even during adversity, willing to go to any means to see them completed.

The Bible tells us that the righteousness of God is revealed from faith to faith (Romans 1:17), meaning that there are various things we will face in our life's journey that will require an element of faith. More importantly, this signifies that there will be more than one thing we encounter in life we will have to complete or see through.

Schools have various levels and even continue to higher forms of education. In order to pursue the next level (whether in elementary or college), I have to focus enough to complete the first task in front of me. This is the challenge that so many have regarding fulfilling their purpose. We associate purpose with meaning or value. Purpose is the course of our entire lives in submission to Christ. The clarification here is that we all have missions to complete or are called to complete, all with different timelines and goals to fulfill. However, our mission is tied to our purpose. Jesus' purpose was to become the Savior of the world. How did he accomplish this? Was it only by dying on the cross? No, He came to free us in many forms through spreading the gospel, displaying miracles, signs, and wonders, and finally, shedding His blood as a sacrificial offering to atone for all sins (futures, past or present).

We believe for one thing as we see God accomplish that in our lives. This encourages us to believe for the next thing. These are missions God empowers us with faith to navigate us in this course of life. If I'm called to be a pastor, there may be a season in my life where I feel compelled to do outreach and ministry. However, there could be another season where I'm drawn towards increasing my knowledge and studying. Both are drastically different but contribute towards the overarching theme of stewardship or shepherding. A pastor who shepherds must be the match to spark the fire for others to believe. This doesn't mean they're exempt from having to navigate through faith themselves and completing missions. No matter our title or position of office, we all must have a heart posture to serve. That's the foundation for completing whatever missions we're called to complete in life. At the heart of every decorated soldier is a heart to serve. The intent of law enforcement is to honor and serve. Every heart of a schoolteacher is to serve the children as best they can with every tool they're equipped with.

Regardless of where we stand in the world with differences of opinion and preferences, we have a common mission to complete what we've been personally assigned to by God and that is to serve one another.

Remember, our Message is not about ourselves; we're proclaiming Jesus Christ, the Master. All we are is messengers, errand runners from Jesus for you.' 2 Corinthians 4:5-6 (MSG)

God equipped us to be dependent on His guidance and instruction. He created, established purpose, and even guides us on how to pursue it. But first we must submit.

> *All we do is trust him enough to let him do it. It's God's gift from start to finish! We don't play the major role. If we did, we'd probably go around bragging that we'd done the whole thing! No, we neither make nor save ourselves. God does both the making and saving. Ephesians 2: 7-10 (MSG)*

As we trust God and His process, He begins to define, 'What Is Our purpose?'

Part 2:
FIVE PILLARS
OF PURPOSE

Five Pillars of Purpose

As we learn our purpose in life, we become equipped with tools to assist us in fulfilling our purpose. Each one of these characteristics upholds us in one way or another. I call them the 'Five Pillars of Purpose.' Each one highlights an aspect of ourselves that we must surrender to God so that he can refine and solidify our purpose. They read as the following:

Self-Worth
Influence
Courage
Identity
Legacy

We often mistake purpose for so many things in life, whether it's our occupations, family roles (parent, husband, brother, etc.), or, more commonly, what others tell us about ourselves. Purpose is often speculative, but for sure, one can conclude that it becomes definitive by your life's pursuit; your passion is most certainly always connected to your purpose. What would you do for free? What drives you? Is there an issue that you feel you were designed to solve? Do you feel that you have an answer to a reoccurring problem that you notice on a grand scale?

It is this train of thought that is so clearly connected to one's purpose. This is why so many can be misled into thinking their purpose is something else in life because of similar interests in so many other things. I may be passionate about politics, but it does not mean that I'm driven to change policies and pursue legislative reform. You may be a parent and have a strong attitude towards bullying against your child, but this does not make you a catalyst for national bullying prevention. My point is that although we experience ambitions, they are often vain or self-seeking. This contributes to the larger issue we have at hand—a bunch of unfinished projects.

How many times have you begun something that you were truly passionate about, then you encountered an issue that you couldn't fix? So often, this can occur, and we walk away. Take, for instance, marriage: one cannot put all the work in for a wedding and simply quit because they're having problems finding a tuxedo. The greater goal is longevity. Sometimes we can't even make it to the ceremony due to a lack of drive. Granted, this analogy may seem abstract, but the meaning behind my example is that we may frequent problems that could be connected to our latter goal (i.e., the marriage example). We may fail to continue due to the hardships presented in the journey ahead.

If my purpose is to end world hunger, then I can't quit because of an absence of donors or improper funding. I must be driven as well as passionate. This dynamic duo can be unstoppable when activated simultaneously. A humanitarian driven to end world hunger, passionate about starving individuals, will not be stifled by lack of support. They will bring change at whatever cost they see fit. The hours, the pay, the support is the last of their concern; solving the problem they feel called to answer is. This is tangible for everyone, but not all achieve this. There have been countless individuals discouraged, defeated, and depleted from all the time, effort, and energy placed into their goals only to see the failure of their contingencies.

When pursuing your goals, structure is needed. Goals are bred out of focus, and one can only have focused and clear goals when they can define their purpose. How do we find our purpose? This is an individual journey, but I can provide you with a strategy on how to unveil your purpose with The Five Pillars of Purpose: Self-worth, Influence, Courage, Identity and Legacy.

What Is Self-Worth?

Why does it matter? Self-worth is connected to our inward perspective and how it impacts our outward ambitions. How do we see who we are and what value do we possess? Although self-worth is largely attributed to one's mental health and other emotional instabilities, it is evident that this is a critical component to the communication strategy of everyone. If one lacks confidence in themselves or feels worthless, chances are that there is a loss of connection to their work and the work they may do on behalf of others. If I don't feel good about myself and what I'm involved in, then how can I care about others and their passions? The short answer is that you don't, and you won't. It's hard to distinguish between enthusiasm and motivation. If we lack drive about something, chances are it will be hard to stay committed to that thing.

Self-worth pertains to every aspect of life and must be established prior to involvement with any subject, goal, or pursuit. If we lack self-worth, then our purpose can never truly be established. How can you establish something that you don't believe in? If you feel that you don't belong, or more importantly, that you don't matter, how can you show even remote interest in interactions with ideas?

There is also a thin line between self-worth and arrogance. Differentiating between the two won't be hard either. Self-worth will frequent a lot of self-reflection and personal improvement along with accountability. Arrogance is a companion of vain glory and selfish ambitions. It can cause you to plummet very quickly and very publicly. Self-worth can advance you very privately and elevate you very quickly.

Why Does Influence Matter?

Influence is an ability that can only exist with the development of an individual's self-worth. If you don't value yourself absolutely, no one will be drawn to your ideas because you won't have anything to offer. How can you establish value to others when you do not value yourself? Influence is establishing value on topics, things, and people. People are drawn to confidence, and confidence can only exist when you are confident about yourself.

Influence is not a negative trait, although negative connotations surround the world of influence. The problematic thing with influence, at times, is those of influence may lack personal accountability. Unfortunately, sometimes the larger your realm of influence, the less accountability you'll be presented with (at least from the spheres you are influencing). Bottom line, without self-worth, there is no influence; and without influence, there is no presence of self-worth or value.

Is Courage Necessary?

Chances are, if you are absent of the first two traits, then courage is not in your rearview. Courage stems from value of self and can be a direct connection of influence as well. We all have an idea of some business or product that would improve if they were challenged, or someone possessed the audacity to implement the change themselves. Often, many missed opportunities of improvement or advancement occur when we don't exhibit the courage to embark upon these opportunities. As you unravel your purpose, you will quickly come to the realization of how important courage is within this journey. You will also know how important it is to prepare to be courageous in order to solidify your purpose to others and, more importantly, to yourself.

Why Focus on Identity?

How do you establish who you are to the common onlooker? This is what I would refer to as your identity. Who do others perceive you to be, and how have they come to this conclusion? Identity is your reputation established through your intentional interactions and opportunities with others. As I alluded to earlier, identity, as well as each other pillar, can only exist if the first thing is in place (self-worth). If you know who you are, then so will others! The same goes for if you know *whose* you are.

For example, if you belong to Bank A and someone comes to recruit you for Bank D, chances are you identify with the guidelines and regulations set in place for Bank A; this is why you decided to identify with that entity over others. How we align ourselves is all determined inwardly and ultimately displayed outwardly. As we internalize the things about ourselves that we deem most valuable, we begin to identify with them and assemble them into our identity.

Identity is not to be mistaken with identifying, although they co-exist. One cannot possess an identity without first understanding how they identify.

What Is My Legacy?

Earlier, we visited self-reflection since, as humans, it's such an innate tendency to reflect. In fact, it's subconsciously etched into our brains to revisit things (sometimes the more traumatic events).

Whether it be a victory, a failure, a dream, or a hard lesson learned, we all in some form or fashion revisit that thing. It's best said that history repeats itself, and to some extent, this may be true. That doesn't mean progression cannot occur in some form. Our tendency to improve ourselves, people, and things lead to our being remembered by others. Why is Beethoven still relevant several centuries later? Because of his ability to reinvent himself through a strength and apply that to his purpose. This is the epitome of a legacy. What can I change that will leave a lasting impression on those to come? Not in a vain way, of course, but how can I eliminate an issue while advancing those affected by the deficits of a problem presented? Once you are able to identify this, you have mastered the strategy of identifying purpose. No longer are you just going to become the 'best' at what you do. How do you effectively eliminate the reoccurrence of the issue that you see in your community, subject, or the person you contend with. It is virtually impossible to leave a legacy without a sense of worth, absence of influence, lack of courage, and certainly, how you identify. Legacy can't be rewritten, but it can be carefully created.

As you visit your purpose and everything related to your ambitions, try to clarify: does this stem from personal preferences, voids within myself, or a battle with my own self-value? If you can answer 'no' to these types of motives, then your purpose will begin to unfold. Draw towards a mentor, leader, or partner that shares a similar passion and begin to observe how they clearly identify what is worth their time, effort, and energy. The key point to fulfilling your purpose is to remain focused. Distractions will come; some are inevitable. Maybe you're a newlywed, a parent, or a caregiver to an elderly parent; whatever the case may be, your pursuit of purpose may be interrupted at times but, if you are determined to stay focused, it will prevail.

Part 3
JOURNAL

What is your purpose?

_____

_____

_____

_____

_____

_____

_____

_____

_____

_____

_____

_____

_____

_____

_____

_____

_____

_____

How do you fulfill your purpose?

_____

_____

_____

_____

_____

_____

_____

_____

_____

_____

_____

_____

_____

_____

_____

_____

_____

_____

Does purpose indicate wealth and riches?

_____

_____

_____

_____

_____

_____

_____

_____

_____

_____

_____

_____

_____

_____

_____

_____

_____

_____

Does identifying your purpose mean the absence of failure?

_____

_____

_____

_____

_____

_____

_____

_____

_____

_____

_____

_____

_____

_____

_____

_____

_____

_____

How do you align your purpose with your profession? Should they both mix?

_____

_____

_____

_____

_____

_____

_____

_____

_____

_____

_____

_____

_____

_____

_____

_____

_____

_____

_____

What do you do when you feel like God identified your purpose, but your plans fail?

_____

_____

_____

_____

_____

_____

_____

_____

_____

_____

_____

_____

_____

_____

_____

_____

_____

_____

_____

ACKNOWLEDGEMENTS

Truthfully, there's one person who deserves acknowledgement for writing this book, and that is the 'Holy Spirit.' I thank God for what he has done through me and in me.

ABOUT THE AUTHOR

Jaquan Kline, a native of the Midwest, has spent several years seeking to advance those within his community and local organizations. Jaquan is driven by the opportunity to champion change in any sphere of influence that he encounters. Over the last few years, Jaquan has committed to developing training workshops that tackle everyday questions we ask ourselves, such as, 'What is your purpose?' Jaquan enjoys spending time with his wife as they are actively involved in ministry and many other local endeavors within the Dallas community. He and his wife happily reside in Dallas, Texas.

website: www.plannedpurpose.org
Instagram: @Plannedpurpose / @jaquankline_
Facebook: Planned Purpose
YouTube: Jaquan Kline